KENNETH LEIGHTON

Crucifixus Pro Nobis

cantata for tenor or soprano solo, SATB & organ

Words by Patrick Carey & Phineas Fletcher

Order No: NOV 070190

NOVELLO PUBLISHING LIMITED

1. CHRIST IN THE CRADLE

LOOK, how he shakes for cold!
  How pale his lips are grown!
Wherein his limbs to fold
Yet mantle has he none.
His pretty feet and hands
(Of late more pure and white
Than is the snow
That pains them so)
Have lost their candour quite.
His lips are blue
(Where roses grew),
He's frozen everywhere:
All th' heat he has
Joseph, alas,
Gives in a groan; or Mary in a tear.

candour] whiteness

2. CHRIST IN THE GARDEN

Look, how he glows for heat!
What flames come from his eyes!
'Tis blood that he does sweat,
Blood his bright forehead dyes:
See, see! It trickles down:
Look, how it showers amain!
Through every pore
His blood runs o'er,
And empty leaves each vein.
His very heart
Burns in each part;
A fire his breast doth sear:
For all this flame,
To cool the same
He only breathes a sigh, and weeps a tear.

3. CHRIST IN HIS PASSION

What bruises do I see!
What hideous stripes are those!
Could any cruel be
Enough, to give such blows?
Look, how they bind his arms
And vex his soul with scorns,
Upon his hair
They make him wear
A crown of piercing thorns.
Through hands and feet
Sharp nails they beat:
And now the cross they rear:
Many look on;
But only John
Stands by to sigh, Mary to shed a tear.

Why did he shake for cold?
Why did he glow for heat?
Dissolve that frost he could,
He could call back that sweat.
Those bruises, stripes, bonds, taunts,
Those thorns, which thou didst see,
Those nails, that cross,
His own life's loss,
Why, oh, why suffered he?
'Twas for thy sake.
Thou, thou didst make
Him all those torments bear:
If then his love
Do thy soul move,
Sigh out a groan, weep down a melting tear.

Patrick Carey d. 1651

4. HYMN

DROP, drop, slow tears,
  And bathe those beauteous feet
Which brought from Heaven
  The news and Prince of Peace:
Cease not, wet eyes,
  His mercy to entreat;
To cry for vengeance
  Sin doth never cease.
In your deep floods
  Drown all my faults and fears;
Nor let His eye
  See sin, but through my tears.

Phineas Fletcher 1582-1650

Time of performance about 15 minutes

CRUCIFIXUS PRO NOBIS

Cantata for Tenor (or Soprano) Solo, S.A.T.B. and Organ

by

KENNETH LEIGHTON, Opus 38

1 CHRIST IN THE CRADLE

Words by PATRICK CAREY

* Hands on separate manuals

His lips are blue____ (Where ro - ses grew),____ He's fro - zen ev-er-y-where:____ All th' heat he has_ Jo - seph,_ a - las, Gives in a groan;____

4

or Ma - ry in a tear._____

2 CHRIST IN THE GARDEN
Words by PATRICK CAREY

7

8

emp - ty leaves each vein.

emp - ty leaves each vein.

emp - ty leaves each vein.

emp - ty leaves each vein.

His

His

f pesante

secco

12

19028

14

19028

16

SOPRANO

tear.

3 CHRIST IN HIS PASSION
Words by PATRICK CAREY

Lento sostenuto, tempo giusto ♩=c. 54
SOLO TENOR (or SOPRANO)

p molto espress.

What bruis - es do I

see!   What hi-deous stripes ____   are   those! ____

Man.* *legato*

* Hands on separate manuals

Could an-y cru - el be e-nough, ____

to give such blows?

Look, how they bind ____ his arms ___ And vex ___

Through hands and feet _____ Sharp nails they beat: _____

sempre sostenuto

SOPRANO

And now the cross, _____ and now the

ALTO

And now the cross, _____ and now the

TENOR

And now the cross, _____ and now the

BASS

And now the cross, _____ and now the

24

26

19028

cross, _____ His own _____ life's loss, _____

nails, that cross, His own life's_ loss,

_ that cross, _____ His own life's loss, _____

nails, that cross, His own life's loss, _____

dim. poco

dim. poco

dim. poco

dim. poco

mf

mf

mf

mf

mp

SOLO *f*

Why, _____ oh, why _____ suf-fered he?

dim. poco a poco

meno mosso, sostenuto e rubato
mf subito
Sigh out a groan,
pp
mp
weep down
(Solo)
ppp colla parte
p
a melt - - - ing tear.
p
rall. ancora
breve
breve

4 HYMN

Words by PHINEAS FLETCHER

Molto adagio, molto sostenuto ma un poco liberamente
pp espress.
poco
p
Drop, drop, slow tears, And
pp espress.
poco
p
Drop, drop, slow tears, And
pp espress.
poco
p
Drop, drop, slow tears, And
pp espress.
poco
p
Drop, drop, slow tears, And
Molto adagio, molto sostenuto ma un poco liberamente
ACCOMPT. (for rehearsal only)
poco
pp espress.
p

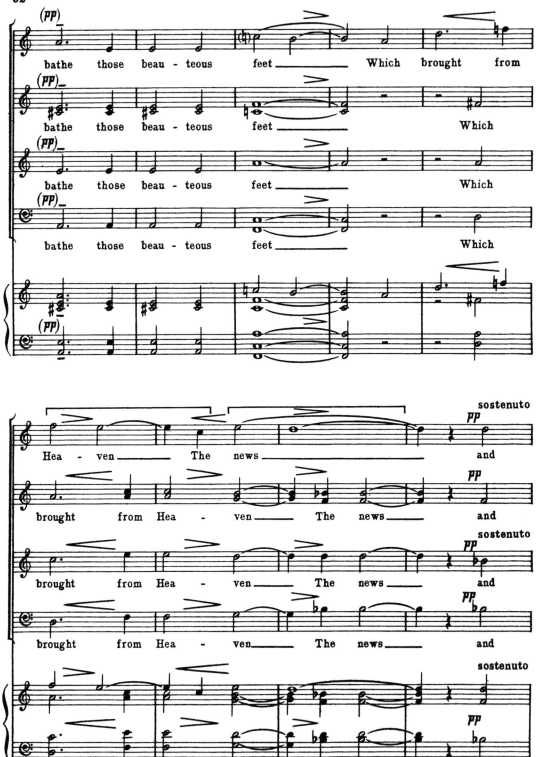

Printed and bound in Great Britain by
Caligraving Limited Thetford Norfolk

4/10(173961)

Anthems for Mixed Voices

Gregorio Allegri	Miserere (Psalm 51)
Peter Aston	A song of the Lord, thy keeper
William Sterndale Bennett	God is a Spirit
Arthur Bliss	Sing, mortals! (St. Cecilia)
William Boyce	O where shall wisdom be found?
William Byrd	Sing joyfully unto God
William Croft	God is gone up with a merry noise
Edward Elgar	The Spirit of the Lord is upon me
Orlando Gibbons	Lord, we beseech Thee
	This is the record of John
Handel	And the glory of the Lord
	For unto us a child is born
Haydn	Insanae et vanae curae
Herbert Howells	Thee will I love
Grayston Ives	Let all the world in every corner sing
John Joubert	O Lord our Lord
	O Lord, the maker of al thing
Bryan Kelly	Out of the deep
Kenneth Leighton	Quam dilecta!
John McCabe	Great Lord of Lords
Mendelssohn	Hear my prayer
Anthony Milner	Send forth Thy Spirit
Hubert Parry	I was glad when they said unto me
Henry Purcell	Funeral sentences
	Jehovah quam multi sunt hostes
	Rejoice in the Lord (The bell anthem)
Martin Shaw	Praise to the Spirit
John Stainer	I saw the Lord
Charles Stanford	The Lord is my shepherd
Christopher Steel	O clap your hands together
John Travers	Ascribe unto the Lord
Thomas Weelkes	Christ rising again
Samuel Wesley	Two motets
Samuel Sebastian Wesley	Ascribe unto the Lord

Approval copies available on request.

904(83)